MOON MANIFEST

TABLE OF CONTENTS

The phases of the **MOON** are the different ways the **MOON** looks from the Earth over about a month. Just like the Earth, half of the **MOON** is lit by the SUN while the other half is in darkness. As the **MOON** orbits around the Earth, the half of the **MOON** that faces the SUN will be lit up. The phases we see result from the angle the **MOON** makes with the SUN as viewed from Earth. The different shapes of the lit portion of the **MOON** that can be seen from Earth are known as Phases of the **MOON.**

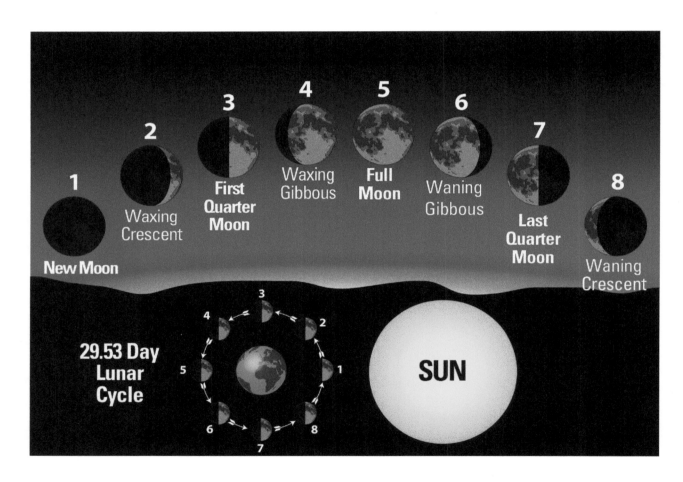

Why Work With The Moon's Phases?

"Whether we move instinctively to the lunar rhythm, or must choose to synchronize ourselves with free will, if we want a broader support for our activities, it makes sense to keep Luna in mind. She offers temporal windows for beginnings and endings, and for everything in between. She is the consummate teacher of process.

New Moon	Intentions are set
Waxing Crescent	Take Action
First Quarter	Grow It
Waxing Gibbous	Refine It
Full Moon	Watch It Bloom
Waning Gibbous	Harvest the Fruit
Third Quarter	Rest & Revel
Waning Crescent	Prepare

First Phase Of The Lunar Cycle – The New Moon

The start of the cycle, where it all begins.

1 - THE NEW MOON (YANG)
- New Beginnings
- Unlimited Possibility
- Planting Seeds
- Intention

~ This is the time for New Beginning and **Renewal**. Plant your **Seed** of **Intention** on what you want to Manifest, and be clear in your **Goal** setting

NEW MOON MAGIC

THE NEW MOON IS A TIME OF LOOKING INWARDS, **DREAMING**, **RESTING**, AND SETTING **INTENTIONS.**
IT IS NOT A TIME FOR **ACTION**, BUT RATHER FOR MAPPING OUT WHAT YOU WANT TO MANIFEST DURING THE NEXT CYCLE. WITHDRAW, GET IN TOUCH WITH YOUR **INTUITION**, AND **PLANT** THE **SEEDS** FOR YOUR NEW DESIRES.

CRYSTALS **FOR THE NEW MOON:**

Moonstone: **The stone of new beginnings // promotes intuition // assists with new energy // protection for a new path** Amethyst: **a stone of deep serenity and enlightenment // neutralizes negative energy // enhances spirituality and meditation**

Aquamarine: the stone of movement // promotes new direction // encourages letting go and going with the flow // reduces fear

NEW MOON RITUALS NEW MOON BATH:

RELEASE AND **PREPARE** FOR THE **NEW MOON** RUN A BATH (take a shower first always take spiritual baths already clean) , LIGHT **3** white **CANDLES** (tea light works well) around the bath, FILL THE WATER WITH HIMALAYAN OR **EPSOM SALT** FOR DETOXIFICATION AND **ESSENTIAL OILS** OF YOUR CHOICE. Also add **Coconut Oil** (or your preferred carrier oil) will leave your body soft as a baby's bottom. Burn your choice of **incense/sage** etc. (remember to command each ingredient's properties even the water what you want it to do. If you have to **SCREAM SCREAM** at it "example: **I Command this water to remove any doubt, negativity from my spirit from my soul from** my body etc. get the point.

ENTER THE BATH AND **VISUALIZE** BEING **ENERGETICALLY CLEANSED** AND **RENEWED** WITH THE ENERGY OF THE **NEW MOON**. **(pour water on your head repeat affirmation of choice always wash down to remove, wash up to bring to you)**

LISTEN TO A GUIDED **MEDITATION**, **INSPIRED MUSIC**, OR SIMPLY **RELAX** IN THE STILLNESS.

STAY IN THE TUB UNTIL ALL OF THE WATER IS GONE, **VISUALIZING** EVERYTHING THAT ISN'T SERVING YOU FROM THE PREVIOUS CYCLE GOING DOWN THE DRAIN.

NEW MOON RITUAL:

PREPARE A QUIET, SACRED PLACE. LIGHT White **CANDLES** AND **INCENSE** IF YOU LIKE. USE **SAGE** OR **PALO SANTO** TO ENERGETICALLY CLEAR YOUR AURA AND PHYSICAL SPACE TO RID IT OF ANY LINGERING NEGATIVE ENERGY.

INVITE DIVINE GUIDANCE IN. (optional) DO AN **ORACLE/TAROT**

NEW MOON SPREAD FOR DEEPER CONNECTION WITH YOUR INTUITION.

CLEANSE & SMUDGE

Releasing and **Clearing** are **Powerful** practices to employ during the **New Moon.** This **Removes** any built up **Negativity** that has accumulated and **Cleanses** the environment and the self for what we are going to have flowing into our lives in the next cycle.

Here is a simple clearing **Blessing** which can be used with any type of **Sacred Smoke** or **Cleansing** method including:

Cedar, **Sweet Grass**, **Sage** or **Herb Smoke**, **Oil Sprays**, or **Salt**.

You can apply this to your room, outdoors, or on **Yourself.**

Write down all of your **Wishes**, **Dreams**, **Intentions**, and **Desires**. Be as specific as you can. Read your list aloud. You can go **Outside** beneath the **Sky** or you can light a **Candle** inside.

Give thanks to the **UNIVERSE**, THE MOST HIGH, **ANCESTORS** (or your chosen dedication) for **Hearing** your **Truth.**

Put in a safe place (bible - under pillow etc.) until the **Full Moon** and then release the Energy in **Sacred Fire** trusting in it coming into your **life.**

You can do this practice with each **New Moon**. Some people choose to **Journal** them and keep them instead of **Burning** them. Do the practice whichever way you are called.

"CLEANSE THIS SPACE, REMOVE ALL ILL; BLESS IT NOW, LET LOVE & LIGHT FILL."

~ARA

NEW MOON MANTRAS & AFFIRMATIONS

New Moon **Affirmations** are potent **Phrases** of **Intent** which you can use to **Anchor** your work during the New Moon. You can say them as a **Blessing**, during your **Intentions**, while you are giving thanks or just on their own as a little mini **Ritual.**

Whatever you decide to do during the **New Moon,** know that this is a time of Cosmic reset and Rebirth.

Take the time you need to **Rest, Replenish**, go Within, **Rework** your **Goals, Dream** your **Dreams** for the **Future** and tap into the **Hope** that **Anything** is **Possible.**

New Moon Blessings,

The **New Moon** brings us the energy of beginnings and is a cosmic refresher. It is a time to leave the past behind and immerse yourself in the Energy **of Rebirth.** Open yourself to **Abundance** and **Possibility** unfolding in your **Life.**

7

NEW MOON MANTRA

I AM RESTORED BY SACRED COSMIC VIBRATION

I AM DIVINELY PROTECTED

I RELINQUISH THE WEIGHT OF THAT WHICH NO LONGER SERVES ME

MY SPIRIT IS AWAKE

MY PATH IS REVEALED

I AM OPEN TO RECEIVE

NEW MOON CHECK

MOON GODDESS DIVINATION

DATE_____ / _____ / _____   #888

PAY TO THE ORDER OF _____ $ _____

_____ DOLLARS

Bank Of The Universe

FOR Abundance, Prosperity & Overflow _____ _____

⑈00888000⑈   3333555544 ⑈   1111 ⑈

(click the image - send an email request for your blank check)

This is a powerful and potent simple ritual for Manifesting Abundance and Prosperity to your life using the Energy of the New Moon each month. New Moon checks are created within 24 hours after the New Moon each month. This harnesses the creative potential that occurs during this Powerful time when we seed what we desire into the Universe.

Second Phase Of The Lunar Cycle – The Crescent Moon

Getting into The Swing of Things… **WAXING MOON,** Getting Bigger and Bright

During the two weeks of the **WAXING MOON**, Luna's light is **increasing** and she's building her form. **CRESCENT MOON** is the time to start **projects** and add actions to the **intentions** you made during the **NEW MOON**. Gather Energies to help you on your way, bring new things, people and relationships into your life, Energy is building

2 - WAXING CRESCENT (YIN)

- Fresh Energy
- Conceptualize
- Focus On Detail
- Sprouting
- Declaration
- What are you feeling led to do?
- What is inspiring you?,
- What do you feel you NEED to do?

Write down and **Communicate** any **Plans** of **Action**, **Ideas** that come to you, in ways that you can begin taking inspired **Action**.
Practice Creativity**.**

Third Phase Of The Lunar Cycle – The First Quarter

This is a time to be Ambitious!

Focus on really accelerating the progress of any projects you're working on, picking up the pace sound in the knowledge of what you're building and working towards. It is essential to make forward strides, really catch onto the **abundant** growing **power** of the moon and the momentum that's underway.

3 - FIRST QUARTER (YANG)
- Momentum
- Challenges
- Paying Attention
- Sending Roots
- Action

~ Keep moving forward and begin putting your ideas and plans into action. This period symbolizes strength, determination, concentration, and commitment. ~

Fourth Phase Of The Lunar Cycle – The Gibbous Moon

➢ **4 - WAXING GIBBOUS (YIN)**
- Patience
- Edit And Refine
- Gestation
- Nurture Your Life

The **GIBBOUS MOON** occurs **3**days before the **FULL MOON**, so we're building up to the time of **fruition** and maximum Energy. The moon will soon be at its peak so now is a time to be **constructive**, adding to what has been building for over a week. We've been allowing the **momentum** of inspired **action** to carry us. Adding to that which we are building. That which we are wanting.

We've learned enough about it to see what is working for it, what isn't, what we like about it, what we don't. We know our feelings about the processes and the outcomes we're getting from it. Now's the time to **refine it.** Follow your **intuition. Your emotional guidance** system. Follow what feels **good**, discard what feels bad but know the difference between bad and difficult. Just because it may feel deterring doesn't mean it's bad.

Example: **Speaking in front of a crowd for the first time**. Know the difference between **discomfort** to **progress** and **discomfort** to let go of Again: What is it that you are wanting? Will this lead you closer to it?

- What needs more attention?
- What parts aren't working?
- Has it led you to something else?
- Are you still focused on the desired outcome?
- Have you become distracted?
- Does it need to be reworked?
- Rethought?

~ This time represents the cultivation of your intentions and ideas. Prepare for manifestation through continued action, creativity, and commitment.

Fifth Phase of The Lunar Cycle – The Full Moon

5 - FULL MOON (YANG)
- Peak Energy
- Blessings
- Joy And Gratitude
- Celebration
- Blossom

Conclusion, Celebration! The Moon Is Biggest And Brightest In The Sky

~ This is the time to push forward the intentions you made during the NEW MOON. Get rid of all negative thoughts, feelings, and emotions that are no longer serving you.

The FULL MOON is a time when we're naturally accelerated, energy is flowing and things will naturally come to a head. Emotions are heightened now, too. It's a great time to give thanks, for the things that have reached fullness, it's a great time to consider that which we can now let go of…

Now your Manifestations are blooming! The fruit of your labor is near! The Full Moon is revealing. It shines light on all of the things we need to know in order to move forward and receive what it is we desire.

The **Moon** is at its most Powerful when **full.** This is when we do our **rituals, spells** and all other **magical** celebrations you may **desire**. We're **Rejoicing** in all of the work we've **done!**

The theme is **"Cleansing-Releasing"**. Write down all of the things standing in between you and what it is you want.

Begin with I **Release**_____ I **Release**_____etc. Write this clause at the end of your list. (I demand that all **Bodies, Programs, Implants, Thoughts, Frequencies, Vibrations, & Patterns** that are enabling, and anchoring the Energy I'm intending to **Release**, to leave me and my energy, through all **space** time and **dimension**, on every layer of my existence You have **NO** place here.........I **declare** all these things to be so and in perfect **alignment** with my **Greatest** and Highest **Good**. So It Is.......... Burn the paper. We're **Releasing** them and their **Hold** on us. Take an **Epsom Salt** bath with **Herbs, Oils, Crystals, & Candles. Relax** into it and **daydream** about how you will feel once what's holding you back is **released.** Think and live in the moment**.**

Full Moon Meditation: I am grateful for things I need to see that have come to light, to the projects that have successfully come to fruition and for the momentum of the moon.

Sixth Phase Of The Lunar Cycle – Waning Gibbous

"The Disseminating Moon"

6 - WANING GIBBOUS - DISSEMINATING (YIN)
- Release + Receive
- Service
- Harvest
- Nurture Other

The **Waning Gibbous** phase is when the fruit will begin to mature. We can begin to see tangible results from the habits we have created.

We're beginning to slow down now and **create space** for our manifestations to come into being. **Self care** and **releasing** are the themes. **Refreshing** and spacious. Opposite of the building and working we were doing leading up to the **Full Moon.** Now we're allowing that which has been set into motion to carry its own momentum.

Enjoy the fruits of your labor.

~ Release and let go of what does not serve you. Absorb all revelations brought forward during the Full Moon and practice gratitude. ~

Seventh Phase Of The Lunar Cycle – The Last Quarter.

7 - LAST QUARTER (YANG)
- BreakDown
- Readjustment
- Transition
- Decomposition
- Forgiveness

This is the second-to-last phase of the **Moon**, and during this time, you want to take those loose ends from the last cycle and really and truly finish up. During the time from the **NEW MOON** to now, you will have become aware of certain things in your life that could be released. The **Last Quarter** gives us fantastic energetic support **release** and **breaks** negative patterns.

➢ ~ Allow the transformation of your accomplishments to fully emerge with **gracefulness.** Continue to let go and release what does not serve you. ~

This is the time for **Rest**. Your work this cycle is **done.** Take some **breathers**. There's nothing left to do but enjoy what you've **created**. More **Self Care** is great. More **Meditation** is great. Wrap up any loose ends

Final Phase Of The Lunar Cycle – The Balsamic Moon / Dark Of The Moon

And Relax, Rest And Retreat… **WANING MOON,** Decreasing, Reducing In Size

8 - WANING CRESCENT - BALSAMIC (YIN)
- Surrender
- Rest And Restore
- Reflection
- Composting
- Intuition

The **Moon** is in its **Balsamic** phase for the **72** hours before **NEW MOON**. During this time it's in its **'DARK MOON'** phase of the **lunar cycle**, and it's a really good window to take time out to **meditate**, **contemplate** and **completely** wind down. **Close off**, really let go and go inward. This is the most **introverted stage** of the cycle and **privacy** is paramount as you clear your head before launch into the new cycle. It's time to get ready for the next phase, the **NEW MOON** when it starts all over again!

DARK MOON Meditation: I am grateful for release from the things I no longer need, for the closing of situations and relationships that no longer serve me and for the power of the universe!

~ Take time to **rest**, **reflect**, **contemplate**, and solidify your **transformation**. This is the final **releasing** and **purging** stage. Prepare **new seeds** to be planted soon. ~

MOON MANIFESTATION

MANIFESTING WITH THE MOON WILL INCREASE THE ENERGY AND POWER OF YOUR MANIFESTATION IF YOU USE THE MOON PHASES TO YOUR ADVANTAGE.......

THE MOON ENERGY ALSO AMPLIFIES OUR EMOTIONS. THINK OF IT AS THE CHANGING TIDES: WHEN ITS FULL, IT CAN BRING ALL OF YOUR FEELINGS TO THE SURFACE.......

JOURNAL PROMPTS
• HOW HAVE I BEEN FEELING?
• WHAT AM I READY TO LET GO OF?

How have I been feeling?

_____
_____
_____
_____
_____
_____
_____
_____
_____
_____
_____
_____
_____
_____
_____
_____
_____
_____
_____

JOURNAL PROMPTS
- ## HOW HAVE I BEEN FEELING?
- ## WHAT AM I READY TO LET GO OF?

What am I ready to let go of?

JOURNAL PROMPTS
- HOW HAVE I BEEN FEELING?
- WHAT AM I READY TO LET GO OF?

What am I ready to invite?

BATH SALTS + OILS• INCENSE/SAGE• ORACLE CARDS• CANDLES • GUIDED MEDITATION• JOURNAL/PAPER SET YOUR INTENTIONS

Helpful New Moon Set Your Intentions

WHAT IS MY INTENTION/S FOR THIS CYCLE?

WHY DO I WANT TO MANIFEST THIS?

WHO ALL WILL BENEFIT FROM THIS MANIFESTATION AND HOW?

THE CORE FEELING THIS MANIFESTATION BRINGS ME:_____

NEW MOON ORACLE SPREAD

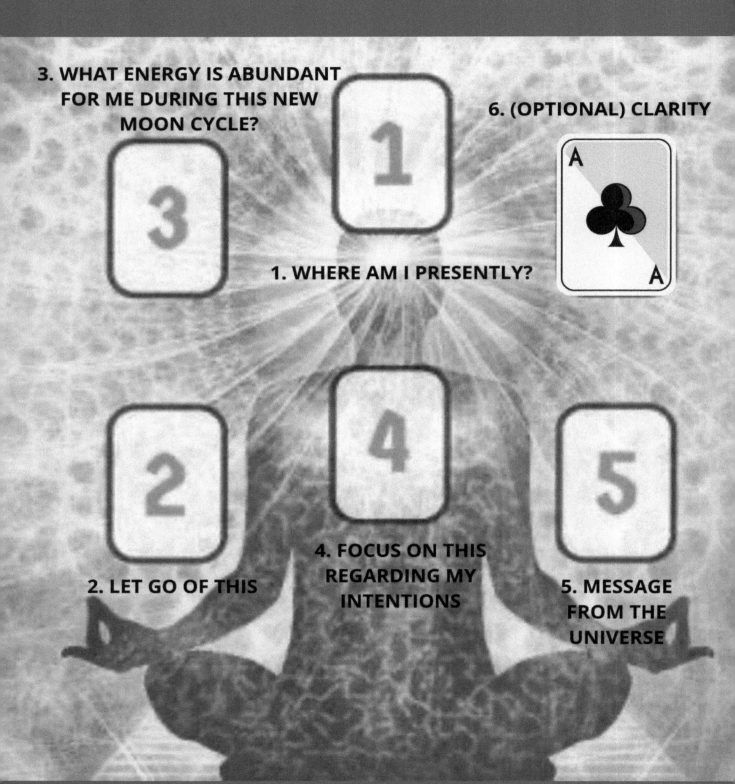

3. WHAT ENERGY IS ABUNDANT FOR ME DURING THIS NEW MOON CYCLE?

6. (OPTIONAL) CLARITY

3

1

1. WHERE AM I PRESENTLY?

2

4

5

2. LET GO OF THIS

4. FOCUS ON THIS REGARDING MY INTENTIONS

5. MESSAGE FROM THE UNIVERSE

WAXING MOON MAGIC

IS A TIME OF AWAKENING AND TAKING INSPIRED ACTION.

YOUR INTENTIONS ARE BEGINNING TO TAKE ROOT AND OPPORTUNITIES WILL BE COMING YOUR WAY. EARLY SIGNS OF MANIFESTATION WILL BEGIN TO APPEAR.
WHAT'S CALLING YOU?
WHAT DO YOU FEEL DRAWN TOWARDS?
ARE YOU IN A STATE OF ALLOWANCE?
IF NOT, WHAT CAN YOU DO TO GET YOURSELF THERE?
CLARIFY - ALLOW - FOLLOW YOUR BLISS
CRYSTALS FOR THE WAXING MOON

Green Aventurine: stone of opportunity // energy of abundance and success // releases old patterns //
Malachite: stone of manifestation + change // absorbs negative energy // balances emotions // promotes taking positive action
Citrine: stone of light // enhances self-esteem // clears negative energy // promotes happiness + attracts prosperity

23

WAXING MOON ACTIVITIES
check-in

SIT IN FRONT OF YOUR SACRED SPACE OR ALTAR AND QUIET YOUR MIND. TAKE SEVERAL DEEP BREATHS AND LIGHT SOME SAGE/PALO SANTO/INCENSE TO ENERGETICALLY CLEAR YOUR AREA IF YOU FEEL CALLED TO DO SO. JOURNAL HOW YOU'VE BEEN FEELING TO RELEASE ANY STUCK ENERGY. READ OVER YOUR NEW MOON INTENTIONS AND CLARIFY THEM IF NEED BE. LIGHT A CANDLE TO ADD ENERGY TO YOUR INTENTIONS AND VISUALIZE CLEARLY YOUR INTENTIONS MANIFESTED.

Follow your bliss

THE WAXING MOON

BRINGS NEW ENERGY AND OPPORTUNITIES. WHAT HAVE YOU FELT DRAWN TOWARDS OR EXCITED ABOUT? WRITE DOWN ANY AND ALL IDEAS THAT COME TO MIND AND ACT ON THE ONES THAT CALL TO YOU THE MOST.

Turbo-Charge The Energy Of Manifestation

FOCUS ON WHAT IS GOING RIGHT TO INVITE MORE OF IT IN: WRITE DOWN AS MANY THINGS AS YOU CAN THAT YOU ARE CURRENTLY APPRECIATING, NO MATTER HOW SMALL.

CANDLES• INCENSE/SAGE•ORACLE CARDS • CRYSTALS• GUIDED MEDITATION • JOURNAL/PAPER

WHAT HAS BEEN GOING WELL SINCE THE NEW MOON?

WHAT DO I FEEL EXCITED ABOUT?

ACTIONS OR THOUGHTS TO LET GO OF THAT ARE HOLDING ME BACK?

CORE FEELING I WANT TO FOCUS ON:_____

WAXING MOON ORACLE SPREAD

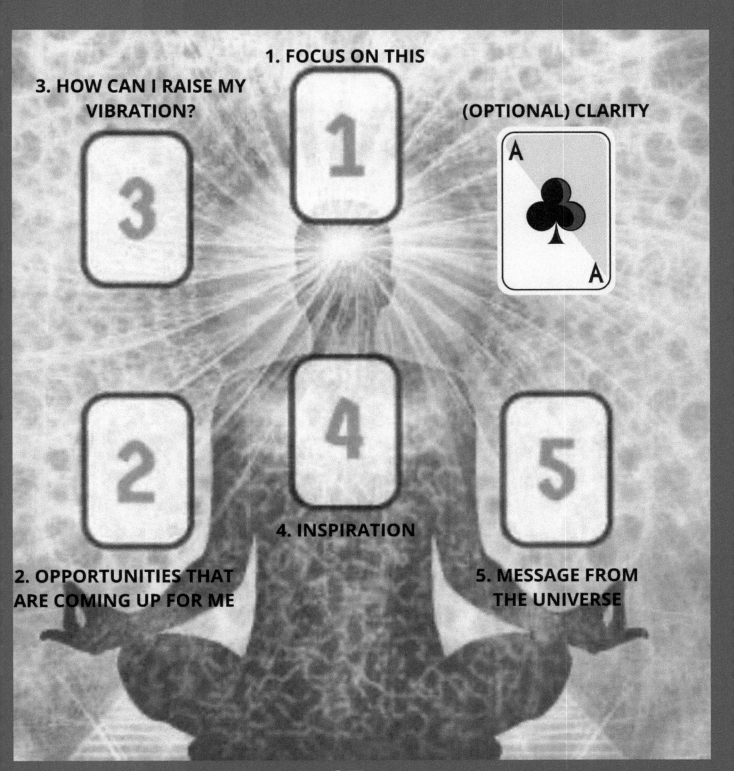

1. FOCUS ON THIS

3. HOW CAN I RAISE MY VIBRATION?

(OPTIONAL) CLARITY

2. OPPORTUNITIES THAT ARE COMING UP FOR ME

4. INSPIRATION

5. MESSAGE FROM THE UNIVERSE

ARE THERE ANY INSPIRED ACTIONS I'M FEELING CALLED TO TAKE TODAY?

DAILY CARD PULL: KEY POINTS

3 WAYS I MOST WANT TO FEEL TODAY:

THANK YOU FOR:

WAXING MOON - ROOT YOUR INTENTIONS

ARE THERE ANY INSPIRED ACTIONS I'M FEELING CALLED TO TAKE TODAY?

DAILY CARD PULL: KEY POINTS

3 WAYS I MOST WANT TO FEEL TODAY:

THANK YOU FOR:

THE FULL MOON:

IS A TIME FOR RELEASING ANY BLOCKS AND SELF-LIMITING BELIEFS THAT HAVE BEEN HOLDING YOU BACK. THE PULL OF THE MOON IS AT ITS HEIGHT DURING THIS PART OF THE CYCLE, SO EMOTIONS CAN BE OVERWHELMING. SELF-CARE IS ESSENTIAL. THINK ABOUT WHAT YOU'VE ACCOMPLISHED IN THE LAST TWO WEEKS SINCE SETTING NEW MOON INTENTIONS; CELEBRATE AND ALLOW YOURSELF TO TRUST AND RECEIVE.

CRYSTALS FOR THE FULL MOON

Peridot: Release + Manifest / **assists in releasi**ng blockages // vibration of increase // stimulates Manifestation

Selenite: a cleansing stone // unblocks stagnant energy // magnifies and cleanses other gemstones // connects to spiritual realm

Moonstone: encourages hope // promotes intuition + feminine **energy** // balances emotions // strong **energy** of **abundance**

FULL MOON RITUALS

Full Moon Release + receive ritual LOOK OVER YOUR NEWMOON INTENTIONS & THINK ABOUT HOW THEY'VE PROGRESSED. WRITE DOWN EVERYTHING YOU'RE CURRENTLY APPRECIATING, NO MATTER HOW SMALL. WRITE DOWN ANYTHING THAT'S COME UP FOR YOU IN THE LAST TWO WEEKS; ANY BLOCKS, SELF-LIMITING BELIEFS, OBSERVATIONS OR LESSONS. TAKE YOUR NEW MOON INTENTIONS & EVERYTHING YOU WANT TO LET GO OF OUT UNDER THE FULL MOON IF THE WEATHER PERMITS. BURN YOUR PAPERS OVER A BOWL & VISUALIZE EVERYTHING BEING RELEASED TO THE FULL MOON, ALLOWING YOURSELF TO FULLY LET GO & NOW RECEIVE.

FULL MOON BATH

Full Moon Bath + Visualization

BRING YOUR MANIFESTATIONS FORWARD WITH THE ENERGY OF THE FULL MOON BY FULLY FEELING INTO THEM. DRAW A BATH WITH EPSOM SALTS TO RECHARGE YOUR ENERGETIC FIELD. SINK INTO THE WATER & VISUALIZE YOUR INTENTIONS FULLY MANIFESTED, NOT THINKING ABOUT THE HOW. SEE YOURSELF THERE; WHAT DO YOU FEEL? WHO IS SHARING IN THIS JOY WITH YOU? HOW ARE YOU CELEBRATING? ALLOW THE BATH TO DRAIN AWAY ANY BLOCKS & THE FULL MOON ENERGY TO AMPLIFY THE POWER OF YOUR VISUALIZATION.

31

JOURNAL PROMPTS
- **WHAT HAS BEEN COMING UP FOR ME?**
- **WHAT HAVE I BEEN LEARNING?**
- **WHAT AM I READY TO RELEASE?**

THE FULL MOON

RELEASE TO RECEIVE

32

_____

_____

_____

_____

_____

_____

_____

_____

_____

_____

_____

_____

_____

_____

_____

_____

_____

_____

_____

RELEASE TO RECEIVE

AMPLIFY YOUR GRATITUDE I'M SO APPRECIATING...

FULL MOON ORACLE SPREAD

1. FOCUS ON THIS

3. DRAW THIS
ENERGY IN

(OPTIONAL) CLARITY

4. WHAT IS EMERGING
FOR ME

2. RELEASE THIS

5. MESSAGE 2.
RELEASE THIS
FROM THE
UNIVERSE

WANING MOON MAGIC

THE WANING MOON IS A TIME FOR ENJOYING WHAT WAS BROUGHT FORWARD THIS LUNAR CYCLE, CELEBRATING YOUR EFFORTS, RELEASING ANY RESISTANCE AND SLOWING DOWN. ALLOW YOUR WORRIES AND ANXIETIES TO FADE AWAY AS THE WANING MOON DOES EACH PASSING NIGHT. REFLECT, REGROUP, DO QUIET ACTIVITIES, AND CLEAR YOUR MIND AND SPACE. TAKE WHAT YOU'VE LEARNED TO PREPARE FOR YOUR NEW MOON INTENTIONS.

CRYSTALS FOR THE WANING MOON

Lapis Lazuli: brings clarity // helps filter what's important and what's not // aids in reflection and understanding

Angelite: brings calm + peace // restores tranquility // protects against negative energies // heightens psychic abilities

Lepidolite: stone of peace // assists in making positive life changes // eliminates stress and anxiety

WANING MOON MAGIC

WANING MOON ACTIVITIES
take stock + regroup

SIT IN FRONT OF YOUR SACRED SPACE OR ALTAR AND QUIET YOUR MIND. TAKE SEVERAL DEEP BREATHS AND LIGHT SOME SAGE/PALO SANTO/INCENSE TO ENERGETICALLY CLEAR YOUR AREA IF YOU FEEL CALLED TO DO SO. THINK BACK TO EVERYTHING THAT WAS BROUGHT FORWARD THIS LUNAR CYCLE AND TAKE NOTE OF IT SO YOU CAN CELEBRATE AND APPRECIATE IT. ALSO NOTE WHAT CAME UP IN THE FORM OF BLOCKS TO BE HEALED. SET AN INTENTION FOR A FEELING TO FOCUS ON THIS WEEK, LIKE FORGIVENESS FOR EXAMPLE, TO HELP AID IN RELEASING THE BLOCK.

Clear + Make Space

RELEASE NEGATIVE ENERGY AND CLEAR YOUR MIND BY GIVING YOUR HOME A GOOD DECLUTTERING AND SCRUB DOWN. ONCE DONE, USE SAGE OR PALO SANTO TO CLEAR THE ENERGY OF YOUR HOME AND YOUR SACRED SPACE AS WELL.

Take Time For Sacred Self-Care

SLOW DOWN THIS WEEK. TAKE BATHS AND DEEP BREATHS. WATCH YOUR FAVORITE SHOWS. RELEASE WHAT HURTS. CONNECT WITH THE DIVINE. REFRAIN FROM TOO MUCH ACTION.

WHAT MANIFESTED FOR YOU OVER THIS LUNAR CYCLE?

WHAT AREAS DO YOU FEEL CALLED TO HEAL?

HOW DO YOU PLAN TO REST + MAKE SPACE FOR YOURSELF THIS WEEK?

CORE FEELING I WANT TO FOCUS ON: _____

WANING MOON ORACLE SPREAD

3. LET GO OF THIS

1. WHERE I AM CURRENTLY

(OPTIONAL) CLARITY

3

1

2

4

5

4. FOCUS ON THIS

2. WORK ON HEALING THIS

5. MESSAGE FROM THE UNIVERSE

THE WANING MOON

CLEARED HOME, CLEARED MIND

Deep Cleaning/Declutter

PAPERWORK
VENTS, FANS, + LIGHT FIXTURES
DOORS
FRONT PORCH/PATIO
BLINDS/CURTAINS + WINDOW
SILLS
FRIDGE + MICROWAVE
PANTRY
KITCHEN CABINETS
SOFAS
LAPTOPS/COMPUTERS (FILES,
PHOTOS, ETC)
LAUNDRY ROOM
CLOSETS + DRAWERS
FLOWERS + PLANTS
CARS
PHONES (APPS, PHOTOS, ETC)
STOVE
RUN VINEGAR SOLUTION THRU
WASHER
OFFICE
WINDOWS
YARD
TOYS
BOOKS/MAGAZINES
GARAGE/SHED
EMAIL/SPAM FOLDERS
WALLETS/PURSES/BAGS
BACK UP PHOTOS

Daily Chores

MAKE BEDS
BREAKFAST
UNLOAD DISHWASHER
LOAD IN THE WASH
DAILY CHORE
DUST / VACUUM / MOP /
BATHROOMS/
ONE DEEP CLEANING ITEM
LUNCH
SWITCH
LAUNDRY/FOLD/HANG
DINNER
DE-CLUTTER
LOAD DISHWASHER
WIPE DOWN KITCHEN
TAKE OUT TRASH

Energetically Clear Space (Choose 2+)

OPEN BLINDS/WINDOWS
CLEAN FRONT DOORSTEP
SAGE ALL CORNERS OF HOME
VISUALIZE CLEARED,
PROTECTED HOME
USE CRYSTALS THROUGHOUT
HOME
CLAP/RING BELL TO SHIFT
ENERGY
TURN ON HIMALAYAN SALT
LAMP
BURN INCENSE/PALO SANTO
CLEAR
CRYSTALS/CARDS/SACRED
SPACE
PLACE SALT IN CORNERS +
ENTRANCE

REST + MAKE SPACE

WHAT CAN I DO TODAY TO HONOR THE STILLNESS AND TAKE CARE OF MYSELF?

DAILY CARD PULL: KEY POINTS

3 WAYS I MOST WANT TO FEEL TODAY:

THANK YOU FOR:

Nov 30th BEAVER FULL MOON

Eclipse In Gemini

NOVEMBER 2020

S	M	T	W	T	F	S
			1	2	3	4
5	6	7	8	9	10	11
12	13	14	15	16	17	18
19	20	21	22	23	24	25
26	27	28	29	30	31	

November is the month to remind us to be thankful for the many positive things happening in our life.

SAINTS DAY PURPLE
NEW NOON YELLOW
FULL MOON RED
THANKSGIVING GREEN
BLACK FRIDAY WHITE

42

Dec 29th COLD FULL MOON

Cancer

DECEMBER 2020

S	M	T	W	T	F	S
1	2	3	4	5	6	7
8	9	10	11	12	13	14
15	16	17	18	19	20	21
22	23	24	25	26	27	28
29	30	31				

Shoot for the MOON even if you miss you will land amongst the starts

NEW NOON YELLOW
FULL MOON RED
CHRISTMAS/KWANZAA GREEN
NEW YEARS EVE WHITE

43

Jan 28th FULL WOLF MOON
Leo

JANUARY 2021

S	M	T	W	T	F	S
					1	2
3	4	5	6	7	8	9
10	11	12	13	14	15	16
17	18	19	20	21	22	23
24	25	26	27	28	29	30
31						

NEW NOON YELLOW
FULL MOON RED
CHRISTMAS GREEN
NEW YEARS EVE WHITE
MARTIN LUTHER KING BIRTHDAY BLUE

44

Feb 27th FULL SNOW MOON

Virgo

FEBRUARY 2021

S	M	T	W	T	F	S
	1	2	3	(4)	5	6
7	8	9	10	(11)	12	13
(14)	15	16	17	18	19	20
21	22	23	24	25	26	(27)
28						

BLACK HISTORY MONTH
NEW NOON YELLOW
FULL MOON WHITE
VALENTINE DAY RED
ROSA PARKS BIRTHDAY BLUE

45

March 28th FULL WORM MOON
Libra

MARCH 2021

S	M	T	W	T	F	S
	1	2	3	4	5	6
7	8	9	10	11	12	13
14	15	16	17	18	19	20
21	22	23	24	25	26	27
28	29	30	31			

NEW NOON YELLOW
FULL MOON RED
WOMEN HISTORY MONTH WHITE
CEASAR CHAVEZ DAY BLUE

46

Anril 27th FULL PINK MOON

APRIL 2021

S	M	T	W	T	F	S
				1	2	3
4	5	6	7	8	9	10
11	12	13	14	15	16	17
18	19	20	21	22	23	24
25	26	27	28	29	30	

NEW NOON YELLOW
FULL MOON PINK
EASTER WHITE
TAX TIME GREEN

47

May 26th FULL FLOWER MOON

Sagittarius

MAY 2021

S	M	T	W	T	F	S
						1
2	3	4	5	6	7	8
(9)	10	(11)	12	13	14	15
16	17	18	19	20	21	22
23	24	25	(26)	27	28	29
30	(31)					

NEW NOON YELLOW
FULL MOON RED
MOTHERS DAY WHITE
MEMORIAL DAY GREEN

48

June 24th FULL STRAWBERRY MOON

Capricorn

JUNE 2021

S	M	T	W	T	F	S
		1	2	3	4	5
6	7	8	9	(10)	11	12
13	14	15	16	17	18	(19)
(20)	21	22	23	(24)	25	26
27	28	29	30			

NEW NOON YELLOW
FULL MOON RED
JUNE 10TH GREEN
FATHERS DAY WHITE

49

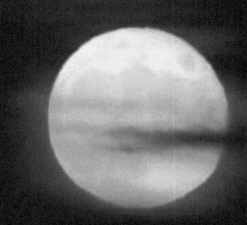

July 24th FULL BUCK MOON

Aquarius

JULY 2021

S	M	T	W	T	F	S
				1	2	3
(4)	5	6	7	8	(9)	10
11	12	13	14	15	16	17
18	19	20	21	22	23	(24)
25	26	27	28	29	30	31

NEW NOON WHITE
FULL MOON RED
INDEPENDENCE DAY BLUE

50

Aug 22nd FULL STURGEON MOON

Aquarius

AUGUST 2021

S	M	T	W	T	F	S
1	2	3	4	5	6	7
(8)	9	10	11	12	13	14
15	16	17	18	19	20	21
(22)	23	24	25	26	27	28
29	30	31				

NEW NOON YELLOW
FULL MOON RED

51

Sept 21st FULL CORN MOON
Pisces

SEPTEMBER 2021

S	M	T	W	T	F	S
			1	2	3	4
5	6	7	8	9	10	11
12	13	14	15	16	17	18
19	20	21	22	23	24	25
26	27	28	29	30		

NEW NOON YELLOW
FULL MOON RED
LABOR DAY WHITE

52

Oct 20th FULL HUNTER'S MOON

OCTOBER 2021

S	M	T	W	T	F	S
					1	2
3	4	5	(6)	7	8	9
10	11	12	13	14	15	16
17	18	19	(20)	21	22	23
24	25	26	27	28	29	30
(31)						

NEW NOON YELLOW
FULL MOON RED
HALLOWEEN WHITE

53

Nov 19th FULL BEAVER MOON
Taurus

NOVEMBER 2021

M	T	W	T	F	S
1	2	3	4	5	6
7	8	9	10	11	12	13
14	15	16	17	18	19	20
21	22	23	24	25	26	27
28	29	30	31			

SAINTS DAY PURPLE
NEW NOON YELLOW
FULL MOON RED
ELECTION DAY WHITE
THANKSGIVING GREEN
BLACK FRIDAY WHITE

54

Dec 19th FULL COLD MOON
Gemini

DECEMBER 2021

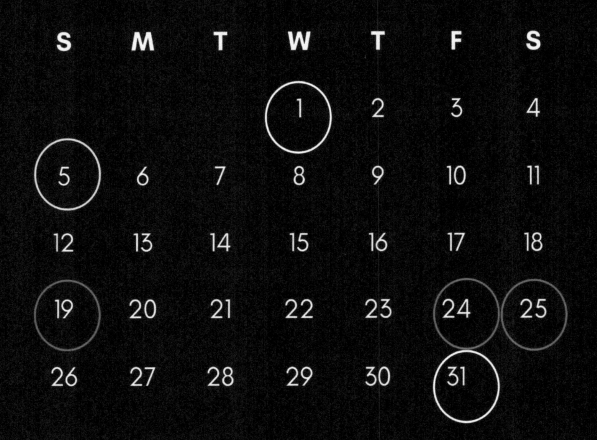

S	M	T	W	T	F	S
			1	2	3	4
5	6	7	8	9	10	11
12	13	14	15	16	17	18
19	20	21	22	23	24	25
26	27	28	29	30	31	

NEW NOON YELLOW
FULL MOON RED
ROSA PARKS DAY WHITE
CHRISTMAS & CHRISTMAS EVE RED
NEW YEARS EVE WHITE

Author: K.S.Scott

Why I created this Moon Manifestation Guide for you.

Today is not about me……… It's about you. How are you doing in life? Are you enjoying every moment? I no…….. I no…….. your thinking who she thinks she is. What makes her the expert? Not saying I'm an expert. I just want to share techniques that have been successful for me throughout my journey.

Whatever your situation is please, do not worry. We all have the power to recreate an amazing life. Boost Manifesting abundance with the Moon Energy, The Moon Energy also amplifies our emotions. Meaning pay attention to your emotions and people around you behavior during certain moon Phases.

I'm excited to take this journey with you. I want to thank you for allowing me the privilege of being a part of your life. In time you will understand the potential this guide has to create positive change in your life. I do have 1 request from you. Please be patient with yourself. Do not expect results overnight. Keep it fun the results will come as you work through

this Moon phase by phase process, while consistently working to better yourself.

I wish you success, love, inner peace, bliss and happiness! Go for it and create the life you desire! Bring your Dreams to life…….

Ig: kre_botanicals

Fb: @meditationoflyfe

https://krebotanicals.com

krebotanicals@gmail.com

YouTube: Moon Goddess Divination

Lightning Source UK Ltd.
Milton Keynes UK
UKHW050836090421
381704UK00003B/15